Letters to Myself...

Mercedes Wright

Presentation by *BookLeaf Publishing*

Web: www.bookleafpub.com

E-mail: info@bookleafpub.com

ISBN: 9789358310092

First edition 2023

DEDICATION

Dedicated to my sister Armani Alexis, Grandma Ruby, Uncle Tony, and my cousin Jamar, my forever angels. I will always be your superstar. I love you.

ACKNOWLEDGEMENT

I cannot express enough thanks to my teachers for believing in my creativity: Ms.Ochoa, my reading teacher; Ms.Rubin, my creative writing teacher; Ms.Castillo, my English teacher; Ms.Medina, my reading coach and all the beautiful women of BLD6 at Hialeah-Miami Lakes Senior High School. I offer my sincere appreciation for the foundation of learning granted by my teachers.

Secondly, I would like to thank the love of my life Devonte Jackson for supporting me through this process and our beautiful daughter Armani Tai Jackson. I love you both so much.

Letter to The Ghetto

The girl that's always been too bougie for the GHETTO folks and too GHETTO for the bougie folks!
I never addressed how I felt until I had to face people around me that challenged my entire existence.
They said things like " Why you look like that?" "Why you sound like that?"
"Yo mama can't afford to buy you that?" or "Oh you know how to draw? But I bet you can't fight!, you won't bust a grape!"
The moment I got any attention for my intellect or my creativity, I immediately became uninteresting, small, and insignificant to society. My society. The GHETTO society.
At least that's what it felt like, the more I tried to relate, I'd get rejected with no explanation, and the more I felt less of myself, the more amplified the humiliation. The feeling to prove I am somebody to a bunch of nobodies festered into a delusion that these people were "IT" and if I wanted to make it I had to get in line!
This was the moment I lost all control of what was left of my self-esteem

Everything I did believe about myself up until that point, got checked at the door and left outside like a bad wig rolling through the night. I could no longer be "ME", but I convinced myself I had to be one of "THEM", to be somebody.

Letter to "ME"

The way I loved "ME" before I walked into the
delusion of proving myself to people who didn't
matter, aw man I miss that love.
I miss telling myself how smart and pretty I was
and complementing my outfits, whew the looks I
put together, ICONIC!
I used to get excited about "ME"!
A beautiful little girl with big dreams and a
smile so wide to fit everything I could see for
myself.
I hugged myself, I prayed for myself & others of
course but most of all I believed in myself.
I pride myself on living life with no regrets.
However, I wish I would have held on to that
love for myself just a little while longer.
Creating an indestructible relationship with my
self-esteem and dignity.

Letter to My Self-Esteem

I gave myself away so much: mentally,
emotionally, creatively and even publicly.
Not understanding my value. I didn't believe I
had any value
I thought if I could be like everybody else I'd
convince people I was worth something.
At home I felt like I was invisible at times.
I began going down the wrong paths to fuel my
self-esteem.
Who knew that would be the start of my worst
nightmare.

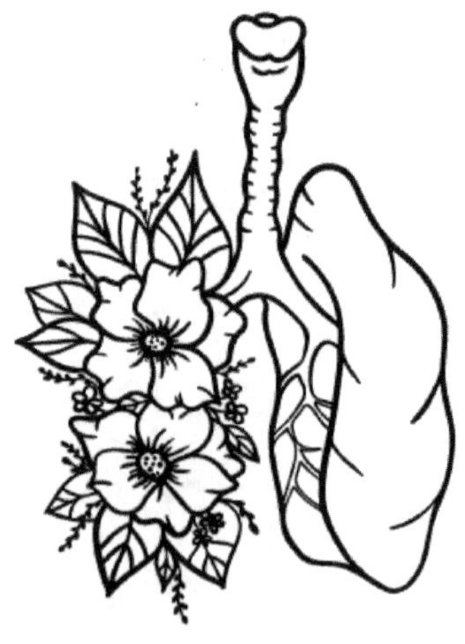

Letter to My Hair

I grew up as a brown girl not loving my hair.
Believing something was wrong with my hair
but not understanding "WHY?"
What was so wrong about my hair?
Why was my hair always "THAT BAD HAIR"?
I had so many questions that spilled over into
answers, leaving imprints on my self-esteem.
Whatever I heard at home and at school is how I
defined my hair.
"You got that bad hair!" or "Your hair shivers up
like carpet!" "Your hair ain't nothing like yo
mama hair!"
I can't lie, I didn't use to feel that way about my
hair but the more I heard it, the more I believed
it. I wanted my hair to be straight all the time,
and not puff up like a chia pet as soon as I
walked out the door. I started thinking the only
way anyone would like me was if my hair was
straight. I would have more friends, get more
attention at home, and I would be the hottest
thang since Lil Mama in a Lip Gloss video.
Trapped in my own mind, waiting for everyone
else's approval.
As time went on the approval never came, and
the opinions wouldn't stop coming.

Letter to My Skin

Too young to wear makeup I had to face a harsh reality when I looked in the mirror. Patches of dry skin, cuts, and scars that turn black the second I touched it. I hated my skin, and didn't like the way I looked. Once I became a teenager in an era where dark skin was unfavorable, I tried every cream, soap, and serum I could find to lighten my skin. Of course, nothing worked, and having unknown allergic reactions that left more marks on my skin, only diminished my self-esteem. I was so tired of hearing " you got bad skin" or " you look sick, you got that s***" on replay in my mind like a bad song. I didn't want to be brown, I didn't want this skin. I wanted to be beautiful.

Letter to My Body

What's wrong with my body? As much as I loved to eat, I could not gain a pound. All my friends and people in my family had curves, and there I was standing with parallel lines for legs. I honestly wasn't jealous of anyone's body. I just wanted to gain weight so I can stop hearing "You look like a skeleton" or "Girl you need to eat a damn sandwich or something". Everywhere I went somebody just had to find a problem with my weight. It made me extremely defensive all the time, and that anger grew into depression. I didn't want to be angry or sad all the time, but I felt like I had to be to protect myself. My body versus everybody else.

Letter to God

I wanted to be close to God, but didn't know where to start. The way people would put me down, I thought something was wrong with me. I started to believe God didn't love me. How could the people he created in his image, be so cruel to me and mask it as love? How could I love them? I wanted to pray it all the way. I was angry at God. Not realizing I was yearning for instant gratification that would never exist. I went through the same pattern for a while. Until I understood, I needed to have faith and learn to love myself first.

Letter to Family

My great-grandmother left an imprint on my mother and I. Keeping the family together with love, food, and classic card games. There was nothing else like it when my family got together. The smell of fried fish, black-eyed peas and freshly baked cornbread filled the air at every family function. All of our day-to-day problems didn't exist and we celebrated our family with a plate of food and my Grandma Ruby's love. She taught us to stick together, love each other, and through any storm in life, we could always eat together. I love you, Grandma Ruby.

Letter to Fashion

"To Wong Foo" made me want big furs, ostrich feather blazers, and luxury luggage to travel the world with my best girlfriends. "America's Next Top Model" showed me what it meant to be fierce! Seeing runways on TV, models in fancy clothes, I knew in my heart that's where I belonged. At six years old I knew I didn't look the part, and I refuse to let that stop me. I was determined to study fashion and become an icon. I had to get there, I had to be "IT", a polished fashion queen.

Letter to Real Love

I always imagined what real love must feel like from another person. My mind went to another place. Dreaming of having a spouse who adores me, cares for me, and thinks I'm the most beautiful girl in the world. I was young but I knew how I wanted another person to make me feel and how to love me. I prayed that God would give me the chance to experience a partner who appreciates me, supports me, one that I can share a life with and have a beautiful family. I didn't need that to happen right away, I just knew I needed it to happen for me and I was willing to give all the love I needed to gain a partner like that.

Love to The Ghetto

Home for me was the ghetto. A place I loved, but it never loved me back. Truth is, where I come from the ghetto don't love nobody back. It's a challenge to exist in that space, but it taught me how to hustle, to understand, my worth, to not allow anyone to stand in my way. The foundation of my identity. I didn't understand it as a kid. In fact, I probably never would have at that age. As tough as my heart and spirit is now, I bust down barriers, not grapes.

Love to "ME"

Seeing myself show up as the woman I've always wanted to be feels so unreal. The relationship I've developed with God has been the best thing that could've ever happened to me. The way I've learned to love myself and all of my flaws it's just like watching a flower bloom and survive through every season. Sometimes I cry thinking about the way I used to treat myself. Then, I remember I didn't have what I have now. The courage to live, the thoughts to keep going, and the forgiveness in my heart to love myself again. This little brown girl has grown into a soft, beautiful, fierce, loving woman. I'm proud of myself. Dammit! I love myself!

Love to My Self-Esteem

Now it's time to pour into my own cup. I spent so much time worrying about unnecessary opinions that didn't matter, and taking care of other people. I had to take some time to build myself up. I know who I am again. I'm not afraid of the unknown anymore. I understand what it means to take care of myself. I got tired of trying to solve everyone else's problems when they didn't want to solve their own. I believe I'm worthy of peace, boundaries, and healthy love. I don't have to settle for it either. My heart feels new, it feels free, and my mind is at ease. I believe in myself and no one can take that away from me.

Love to My Hair

I dreamed about this for a long time. The days I started to love and appreciate my hair. My thick jet-black curls and soft edges. Don't get me wrong, it's still a whole project to wash and blow dry my hair, but I enjoy every minute of my self-care. My freshman year of college, I learned how to cater to my crown. Attending an HBCU, I discovered the importance of being a brown girl with thick, bold, beautiful hair. The appreciation for black hair made me confident in my power and I truly felt comfortable wearing my natural hair. I didn't wait for anyone to define my hair for me. Once I canceled out all the noise, I found my inner voice, and I finally saw my crown. I love my hair.

Love to My Skin

I now realize the essence of my skin. I love being a brown girl. Through my flaws, I've learned how to nurture my skin. In reality, people are always going to judge me, and gossip about my blemishes and imperfections. The greatest part about that for me is that it doesn't disrupt my love for my skin anymore. I no longer have the desire to change anyone's opinion, that's between them and whoever is miserable enough to listen. I'm cozy, and I love it here. Even when I get stubborn scars or dark spots on my face, I love what I see when I look in the mirror. I wish all those same people who despise my skin, the courage to love their own.

Love to My Body

Honey, if all you petite haters could see me now! I'm still small, only this time, baby them parallel lines are given the girl's petite parentheses and I love it! Only time I'm concerned about my weight these days is to better my health. Otherwise, I eat what I want and I look damn good while doing it. I'm not here to body shame anyone, I just hope every last one of you that made it your business to have a problem with my body, looks their absolute best. See I've learned to live out loud and appreciate the way I was created. Life is much more peaceful for me that way. As long as I'm healthy, and I can serve unforgettable looks in fashion, my body is all right with me.

Love to My Family

Family means everything to me. The values my grandmother instilled in me made me want to have my own family someday. I believe in caring for the people I love. They deserve the best version of me, happy me, healed me. God blessed me with a tribe of my own that has been more than I could ever ask for in a family. A man that I can pray to God with through any season, and watch all my favorite tv shows with in our pajamas. A beautiful healthy daughter that lights up a room wherever she goes. My parents are healthy, always happy to spend time with us and they are amazing grandparents. I host my own family functions, cook food with all my heart and soul to watch everyone enjoy. The feeling I get when I see my love brings my family together gives me joy I never thought I needed.

Love to God

God knows me better than I know myself. Life has hit me harder than a mouse trap, but the favor God has over my life has been like no other. I pray in every season and God carries me through each and every time. I would never tell anyone how to pray, or who to believe in spiritually. There's just no way I can deny God. He has done so many remarkable things for me, that I could've never imagined. I've seen miracles and dreams manifest right before my eyes that I know in my heart could only be God's plan. God, I express my gratitude and appreciation for all the experiences you have given to me. I know the best is yet to come. God, I thank you for everything that I am and everything that I have in this life and the next. I love you.

Love to Fashion

I surprise myself every time I put a look together and pose for a photo. I'm the "IT" girl I've always wanted to be since I was six years old. The best part about my style is no matter what it costs I can make anything look good. I can turn five dollars into five hundred with one look. I learned how to be "THAT GIRL" no matter what my bank account looks like at the moment. I could have not a dollar to my name but I bet you I look like a million bucks honey! Oh and best believe my bills are paid! When I look good, I feel good. As I've gotten older, I realized in this life only one thing is for sure, life is short I want to enjoy every moment I have contributing to fashion. I'm here for a good time not a long time. I'm making every look ICONIC!

Real Love: A Dream Come True

I thought love like this only existed in the movies. This may sound cliche but having someone that loves you for you and honors who you are as a person is truly one in a million. Yet, God gave me my golden ticket. A man with substance, values, dedication, gratitude, and a consistent love. I have a built-in best friend that I can have uncomfortable conversations with and the love, respect and honor doesn't change. The storms we've faced have held us together through it all. We create our silliest moments together. Dancing, singing or irritating each other. We find a way to spend time to enjoy each other no matter what's going on in life. Experiencing this level of peace in a relationship has been a dream come true and our love has granted us a bigger blessing. Our beautiful daughter that gives us an overwhelming amount of love each day. Our bond, our connection created a beautiful human being. I tell God all the time, this love was well worth the wait. Thank you.

Beautiful Love Letter to My Daughter

Armani Tai Jackson, baby you are mommy's happily ever after. The love in your smile when you look in the mirror and see yourself, is God reassuring me, that you know your value. Your laugh is the same song I want to listen to every day on repeat, and your heartbeat at the top of the charts every night. No one can ever tell you how much I love you, but I hope this letter can spell it out for you. Armani you make mommy's world so peaceful when you look at me. When I'm afraid, hurt, or angry, it's you who brightens my day. Even when you've called my name, a thousand times "mommy, ma-maaaaaa, ma!, mommyyyy" I still want to hear your voice and see that smile. You have a light inside of you that shines like no other star I have ever seen baby. Thank you for sharing that light with me every day and being mommy's superstar. I love you french fry!

www.ingramcontent.com/pod-product-compliance
Lightning Source LLC
LaVergne TN
LVHW050249200726
843509LV00015B/2950